EXPLORING AWESOME ANIMAL BODIES WITH MATH

Robyn Hardyman

PowerKiDS press™

New York

Published in 2017 by
The Rosen Publishing Group, Inc.
29 East 21st Street, New York, NY 10010

Cataloging-in-Publication Data

Names: Hardyman, Robyn.
Title: Exploring Awesome Animal Bodies with Math / Robyn Hardyman.
Description: New York : PowerKids Press, 2017. | Series: Math attack: exploring life science with math | Includes index.
Identifiers: ISBN 9781499431179 (pbk.) | ISBN 9781499431193 (library bound) | ISBN 9781499431186 (6 pack)
Subjects: LCSH: Animals--Adaptation--Juvenile literature. | Adaptation (Biology)--Juvenile literature.
Classification: LCC QH546.H349 2017 | DDC 591.4--dc23

Produced for Rosen by Calcium
Editors for Calcium: Sarah Eason and Jennifer Sanderson
Designers for Calcium: Paul Myerscough and Jennie Child
Picture researcher: Rachel Blount

Picture credits: Cover: Shutterstock: Joe Belanger tl, Peter Waters r; Inside: Shutterstock: Andrey Armyagov 15, Atiger 6, Photocreo Michal Bednarek 20, Ramon Carretero 12, Cbpix 1, Paisan Changhirun 19, 21t, Yanik Chauvin 23, EcoPrint 8, Efendy 11, 28t, Dirk Ercken 16, Frolova_Elena 26, Fred Goldstein 14, Guner Gulyesil 10, Attila JANDI 27, 29b, Images by Dr. Alan Lipkin 24, Alberto Loyo 17, Nataliia Melnychuk 21, Jonathan Pledger 5, Ondrej Prosicky 9, 28b, Rokopix 25, Harshvardhan Sekhsaria 18, Vanchai 4, Vlad61 13, Worldswildlifewonders 7, Feng Yu 22.

Manufactured in the United States of America
CPSIA Compliance Information: Batch #BW17PK: For Further Information contact Rosen Publishing, New York, New York at 1-800-237-9932.

CONTENTS

A WORLD OF ANIMALS

The natural world is full of the most incredible animals. Animals have amazing bodies that are brilliantly designed to suit the places where they live, to find food, and to stay alive.

Animal Groups

Scientists divide the animals of the world into groups according to their features. Within each group there are thousands of different **species**, or types, of animal. There are two main groups of animals: vertebrates and invertebrates. Vertebrates are animals with a backbone and a skeleton of bones. They include mammals that feed their young with milk, birds, fish, reptiles such as snakes, and amphibians, which are creatures that can live both on land and in water. Invertebrates are animals with no backbone or skeleton. About 97 percent of all animals are invertebrates. They include insects, spiders, worms, snails, and **crustaceans** such as crabs.

Crabs are invertebrates that live in the sea. Their hard shells give them protection.

Move and Protect

Having a skeleton of bones allows vertebrates to grow big, because their skeletons support their bodies as they move. Invertebrates are generally smaller, and many species live in the sea, where their soft bodies are supported by the water. Some invertebrates have a very hard outer layer to protect them. Crabs and snails have shells, for example. Insects have a hard, outer skin. Most invertebrates hatch out from eggs, and many of them change shape as they develop into adults.

MORE THAN A NUMBER!

MORE THAN 1.2 MILLION SPECIES OF ANIMALS HAVE BEEN IDENTIFIED SO FAR, AND THOUSANDS OF NEW SPECIES ARE DISCOVERED EVERY YEAR. WE KNOW OF ABOUT 6,000 SPECIES OF AMPHIBIANS, 10,000 BIRDS, 30,000 FISH, 5,000 MAMMALS, 8,000 REPTILES, 40,000 CRUSTACEANS, AND 950,000 INSECTS.

MONKEYS AND APES

Our closest relatives are monkeys and apes. Monkeys and apes are **primates**, and so are human beings. Monkeys have tails, while apes, such as chimpanzees and gorillas, do not. Lemurs and bush babies are primates, too. The bodies of all primates are perfectly designed to suit their **habitats**.

Very Smart

Primates are smart. They have large brains so they have developed some complex skills to help them survive. Chimpanzees cannot speak, but pull faces and make sounds to communicate with each other. Their faces are bare of fur and their eyes are clearly visible to make this easier. Chimps' hands have thumbs to help them handle "tools" to solve problems, such as picking and opening fruit and finding insects to eat. Usually, apes live mostly on the ground, but orangutans and gibbons spend a lot of their time in the trees.

Chimpanzees can express their feelings clearly on their faces.

Life Above Ground

Primates that live in the trees need strong arms and legs for climbing. Monkeys often have strong tails, too. These help them hang onto branches and balance as they move around. Sometimes, their tail is even longer than their body. The smallest monkey is the pygmy marmoset: an adult weighs just 3.5 ounces (100 g).

MATH ATTACK!

The golden lion tamarin is a beautiful, golden monkey with long hair on its face, like a lion's **mane**. It lives in the rain forest. So much rain forest has been destroyed that this monkey has become very rare. Only about 400 are left in the wild. If 20 golden lion tamarins die every year and no more are born, how many years will it take until they have disappeared? Use this calculation to help you solve the problem:

400 TAMARINS ÷ 20 TAMARINS EACH YEAR = ? YEARS

BIRDS

Birds live all over the world, in a dazzling variety of species. They are some of the most colorful creatures on Earth. They fly to find their food, to escape from danger, and to find a safe place to live. They all have wings and, for most of them, that means they can go soaring up into the air.

The shape of a bird's wing is perfect for take-off and flight.

Designed for Flight

The bodies of most birds are designed for flight. They are light and strong. Their bones are hollow, or filled with air, which makes them light. Their strength comes from muscles in their chests that pull their wings up and down. Birds' wings are curved on top and hollow underneath, which is a good shape for lifting them off the ground. The size and shape of the wings affects how a bird flies. Long wings are better for gliding, while pointed wings are better for speed.

Beautiful Display

Birds can be some of the most showy animals, too. **Birds of prey** spread their enormous wings. Other birds, such as peacocks, put on displays of their colorful feathers to impress a mate. The male birds are often more colorful than the females, for the same reason. Some birds are very loyal to their mate when they find it. Many kinds of penguins keep the same mate for life. Puffins do this, too. The males and the females both work on making the nest and looking after the chicks when they hatch. This behavior is not seen in many animals.

Hummingbirds beat their wings 12 to 90 times per second as they hover in the same place. This is so fast it makes a humming sound.

MORE THAN A NUMBER!

SOME BIRDS ARE INCREDIBLY STRONG. THE EAGLE IS THE STRONGEST BIRD. IT CAN LIFT SOMETHING 4 TIMES ITS OWN BODY WEIGHT AND CARRY IT ALONG AS IT FLIES.

eagle

INSECTS AND BUGS

There are more insects on Earth than any other kind of animal. They are amazingly varied and they can live almost anywhere. All insects have six legs and three parts to their body: the head, **thorax**, and **abdomen**. Spiders are not insects because they have eight legs.

Flying High

Many insects can fly. They usually have two pairs of delicate wings that allow them to fly swiftly in any direction. Their legs are divided into sections so they can bend, and their eyes are made up of many smaller eyes joined together. This gives them superb vision. Insects also need weapons for attack and defense, and they have some truly awesome ones. Some, such as wasps, bees, and scorpions, use stings. Others, such as the prickly thorn bug, have spikes, or long horns like the enormous goliath beetle.

This is a moth, not a bird! The hummingbird hawk moth looks like a hummingbird and it makes a similar sound, too, as it flaps its beautiful wings.

The dung beetle is the strongest animal on Earth. It can pull 1,141 times its own body weight in dung!

All Change

Many insects change their shape as they grow up. The dragonfly hatches from an egg as a nymph. It has no wings and lives in water. Gradually it sheds its skin, or molts, several times, changing shape each time until it is an adult with wings. Cockroaches do this, too. Butterflies change even more. They hatch as creeping caterpillars, then hide inside a tough **pupa** for a few weeks. The adult butterfly then hatches from the pupa, complete with colorful wings! This process of change is called metamorphosis.

MATH ATTACK!

There are more than 12,000 species of ants around the world. They live in large groups, or colonies, and they work together on tasks such as finding food. There can be millions of ants in a single colony. Ants are incredibly strong and can lift objects 20 times their own weight. That is like a small child being able to lift a car! Imagine a giant ant weighed 18 pounds (8 kg). What would be the maximum weight that it could lift? Use this calculation to help you solve the problem:

18-POUND ANT X 20 = ? POUNDS MAXIMUM WEIGHT

FISH

The world's oceans and rivers are filled with fish with extraordinary bodies that are designed to help them feed, move, and survive. Some fish live in oceans, while others live in freshwater habitats, such as rivers and lakes.

The terrifying great white shark has large gills and rows of super-sharp teeth to slice into its **prey**.

Perfect Swimmers

Fish are designed for swimming. Their bodies are **streamlined** so they can travel easily through water. Most fish are pointed at the front and smooth on the outside. Their body is strong and muscular so they can bend into curves to push forward through the water. Their fins help them steer. They can live underwater because they breathe through slits in their sides called gills.

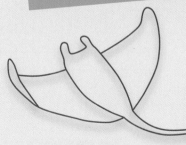

manta ray

Flat but Fast

Some fish are not long and thin, but flat. It suits flatfish to be flat because they live near the seabed. They use their fins to sweep the seabed, disturbing the sand and stones, which fall over them and hide them from **predators**. Rays are a kind of flatfish. They have large side fins and long, thin tails. Manta rays "fly" underwater like giant birds, flapping their fins, and they can leap up to 6 feet (1.8 m) out of the water.

Tropical fish come in many shapes, sizes, and wonderful colors.

MORE THAN A NUMBER!

THE COELACANTH CAN GROW TO 6 FEET (1.8 M) LONG, WEIGH ABOUT 200 POUNDS (91 KG), AND LIVE FOR 60 YEARS. IT FEEDS MOSTLY AT NIGHT. COELACANTHS HAVE LOOKED THE SAME FOR ABOUT 400 MILLION YEARS. THIS MAKES THEM ONE OF THE OLDEST FISH.

SEA CREATURES

The oceans are teeming with creatures other than fish, too. Some are enormous, like whales, while others are tiny, like sea slugs.

Whales

Whales look like fish, but actually they are mammals that give birth to live young and feed them with milk. They cannot breathe underwater. They come up to the surface and breathe through blowholes on top of their heads. Their tails are flat and made of two parts, called flukes. Narwhals are remarkable whales because the males each have a long, spiraled tooth projecting from their head, like a horn. This can be up to 10 feet (3 m) long. Males use these teeth to fight other males or to attract females. Dolphins and porpoises are also types of whales. Their bodies are streamlined to swim very fast to escape predators such as sharks.

Sea otters hold hands when they sleep. This is to keep them from drifting apart on the water.

So Much Variety

In shallow, warm waters, the sea is full of brightly colored creatures. Sea stars, for example, have long, flexible arms for settling on rocks. If an arm breaks, it will grow back again. Under their arms are rows of tiny, tube feet. These press onto surfaces to help the sea stars creep along. The biggest shellfish is the giant clam, which can be 3 feet (1 m) across. It can grow a pearl inside as big as a golf ball. Sea slugs are little splashes of color in the shallow sea. Their bright colors warn predators that they contain poison. Squid and octopuses use their long **tentacles** to zoom along.

The Japanese spider crab is enormous. It can measure 12 feet (3.7 m) across its front claws.

MATH ATTACK!

narwhal

A male narwhal is about 5 feet (1.5 m) long when it is born and it can grow to 20 feet (6 m) long. How much longer is the adult than the newborn narwhal? Use this calculation to help you solve the problem:

20 FEET – 5 FEET = ? FEET

FROGS AND SNAKES

Frogs and toads are amphibians and they can live on land and in water. Snakes are reptiles, and so are turtles and crocodiles. Reptiles are **cold-blooded** so they need to warm up each day by sitting in the sunshine.

The cane toad has large, bulging eyes to look out for danger. It has a sticky tongue for catching insects and worms to eat.

How Do They Do It?

How can amphibians live on land and in water? Their incredible bodies are adapted to make this possible. They breathe through their noses and also through their cold, wet skin. Their feet are **webbed**, which helps them swim. Frogs start life as eggs in water. They hatch out as tadpoles, with long tails for swimming. Slowly, they grow legs and hop onto land.

Frogs and toads also have an amazing range of skin colors and markings. Some colors and markings help them blend in with their surroundings. This is called **camouflage**. Other colors warn that an amphibian is poisonous or help it attract a mate.

Scary Snakes

Snakes come in all sizes but the biggest are not necessarily the deadliest. Some snakes, such as anacondas and pythons, kill their prey by squeezing it to death in their strong coils. Anacondas can be more than 16 feet (5 m) long. Others, such as vipers and rattlesnakes, poison their prey with sharp **fangs** and then eat it. Snakes do not have chewing teeth, so they swallow their prey whole. Their jaws are specially designed to open very wide to make this possible. Snakes are not slimy. Their bodies are covered with dry scales, which bend as they move.

MORE THAN A NUMBER!

THE LONGEST SNAKES IN THE WORLD ARE RETICULATED PYTHONS. THEY LIVE IN SOUTHEAST ASIA AND THEY CAN BE 21 FEET (6.4 M) LONG, OR MORE. THESE SNAKES ARE NAMED FOR THE DIAMOND-LIKE PATTERN ON THEIR SKIN.

The body of this python has stretched to fit around the body of the small deer that it has just eaten whole.

HUNTERS

All animals must eat to stay alive, but some creatures are built to kill. Their bodies are perfect for locating their prey and killing it effectively. Mammals, fish, birds, insects, and many other kinds of animals can be predators.

The tiger is a perfectly designed killing machine.

Killer Design

To be a successful hunter, an animal needs good senses, such as sight, hearing, and smell, to find its prey. It then needs speed or cunning to catch it, and weapons for killing it. This deadly combination comes in a remarkable variety of forms. Tigers have speed and power to chase their prey, and terrifyingly sharp teeth to kill it. Their huge front paws knock over the prey and hold on tight. Even their tongues are designed for the job. Their rough surfaces are perfect for licking meat off skin and bones.

Different Tactics

Many spiders sit still and wait for their prey to come to their traps: the sticky webs of silk they weave. Eagles and owls soar quietly through the sky on powerful wings and swoop down to crush their prey in their talons, or claws. Wolves work together in a pack to surround prey that is bigger than them, such as deer. They kill the prey and share it. The scorpion has the perfect weapon for its hunting: a posionous stinger on the end of its tail, which it uses to stab its prey.

The strong jaws and sharp teeth of crocodiles are perfect for snapping up fish and bigger animals.

MATH ATTACK!

The snakehead fish is a deadly hunter found in lakes and rivers. It is 5 feet (1.5 m) long and, unusually for a fish, it has long, sharp teeth and it can breathe air. It eats fish, birds, and other small animals. Its small head is covered in scales, which make it look like a snake. Imagine a snakehead fish eats 3 fish, 1 bird, 1 mouse, and 2 insects in a week. How many animals will it have eaten in 5 weeks? Use this calculation to help you solve the problem:

3 + 1 + 1 + 2 = ? ANIMALS X 5 WEEKS = ? ANIMALS EATEN

CATS

The male lion looks very fierce with his large mane, but the females do most of the hunting.

They may be big cats in the wild or pets in our homes, but whatever their size, cats are impressive animals. There are more than 40 species of cat in the world, but they all have features in common. They are excellent hunters, with sharp teeth and claws to kill their prey. They have powerful senses, too. They can hear the smallest sounds and see a moving target from a distance.

Big Cats

The big cats include the lion, tiger, jaguar, cheetah, and leopard. They are all skillful hunters, intelligent, and powerful. These cats can roar but they cannot purr. Like all cats, they walk on their toes, and the thick pads on their feet help them stay silent as they creep up on their prey. Lions live in a family group, called a pride. In each pride, there is a male, several females, and their cubs. The male has a thick mane of fur to make it look even more scary.

Small Cats

Small cats live in many kinds of habitats and are adapted to suit each one. The bobcat hunts rabbits and hares in woodlands and open areas. The sandcat lives in the desert. Thick furry pads on its feet allow it to run over the soft, hot sand. The puma, or cougar, lives in mountains and rain forests. It has strong back legs for climbing and jumping, and large paws to hold down its prey.

MORE THAN A NUMBER!

AN ADULT MALE LION CAN EAT AROUND 95 POUNDS (43 KG) OF MEAT AT 1 MEAL. IT ROARS TO PROTECT HIS TERRITORY FROM OTHER MALES, AND ITS ROAR CAN BE HEARD UP TO 5 MILES (8 KM) AWAY. ITS PRIDE MAY HAVE UP TO 40 LIONS IN IT.

The lynx's thick fur keeps it warm, and its wide feet keep it from sinking into the snow.

NIGHT ANIMALS

For many animals, the night is their time to shine. They come out at night for different reasons. For some, the dark allows them to hide from their enemies. For others, the night is a relief from the blazing heat of the day. For the hunters, the night is the perfect time to swoop down on a meal without being seen.

Seeing and Hearing

With little light to help them, **nocturnal** creatures need to have very good senses. Many have special eyes and other developed senses to help them survive. Cats and snakes, for example, have eyes that can open very wide to let in as much light as possible. Snakes also use their tongues to sense the smell of prey in the air. Some of the most amazing night animals are bats. They find their way around by making very high squeaks and listening for the echoes as they bounce off nearby objects. They catch insects in their open mouths as they fly.

The great horned owl is a stealthy nocturnal predator. Its huge eyes let in a lot of light. It can catch prey as big as a Canada goose.

The big ears of the fox work like funnels to catch as many sounds as possible in the quiet of the night.

Feeling

Some animals feel their way around in the dark. Cockroaches have hairs on their bodies to pick up the sounds of danger in the dark. That is why they can disappear long before you switch on a light. Pit vipers sense the hot bodies of their prey in the dark using heat pits under their eyes. Moths, such as the Atlas moth, have feathery **antennae**, or feelers, on their heads. They use these to pick up the scent of a female.

bat

MATH ATTACK!

There are more than 1,000 species of bats in the world. Some eat fruit; others eat insects or larger prey, such as frogs and fish. A few species drink blood. These are called vampire bats. A vampire bat drinks about 4 teaspoons of blood a night. How many teaspoons of blood would it drink in 3 weeks? Use this calculation to help you solve the problem:

7 DAYS A WEEK X 3 WEEKS = ? DAYS
? DAYS X 4 TEASPOONS = ? TEASPOONS

FINDING A MATE

One thing is essential for every species in the animal kingdom, and that is to make sure their species continues. Some animals go to great lengths to find a mate so they can reproduce and have offspring.

Dancing and Prancing

Very often it is the males who show off to attract a female, who then judges their performance. The males can do this in many ways. Male peacock spiders have an impressive plan. They are brightly colored in blues, yellows, and reds, and when they spot a female, they start to dance. They wave their legs up in the air in rapid, jerky moves. Male guppy fish do something similar. They have long, colorful tails that swirl about beautifully as they twist and turn in the water, to persuade a female to mate.

Showing Off

Frigate birds are among the most dramatic show-offs of all. They can blow out their throats into huge, red, heart-shaped balloons. The male bower bird has a different approach. It builds a nest to show a female it is serious about raising a family. The male builds and decorates the nest with great care to impress the female.

The female frigate bird chooses the male with the most striking display.

The male peacock puts on a fantastic display of its tail feathers to attract the peahen.

Mating for Life

Most animals do not keep one mate for life, but some species do. Swans stay together all their lives, and the male helps with nest-building. Other birds, such as albatrosses and sandhill cranes, are loyal in this way, too. Both species dance together and have special calls for each other.

swans

MORE THAN A NUMBER!

ONCE A PAIR OF BALD EAGLES HAS FOUND EACH OTHER, THE BIRDS STAY TOGETHER FOR LIFE. EVERY YEAR, THEY RETURN TO THE SAME NEST, WHICH THEY REPAIR AND ENLARGE. AFTER MANY YEARS, THE NEST CAN BE UP TO 6 FEET (1.8 M) ACROSS AND 8 FEET (2.4 M) DEEP.

AWESOME BODIES

The seahorse is an unusual-looking fish. It swims upright and can change color to match its surroundings, to stay safe.

From tiny insects and sea sponges to huge lions and vultures, animals come in all shapes and sizes. All animals have some features in common. They can breathe and move around, they can find food to give them energy, and they can reproduce to ensure their species survives. The ways in which they do this, however, are incredibly varied and wonderful.

Staying Alive

Whether they have fur, feathers, or scales, animals are perfectly suited to the habitats they live in. They may have wings to take them up into the air or fins to help them swim in the ocean. They may be strong and super-speedy to catch their prey, or silently sneaky to lie in wait for a meal to pass by. Some animals defend themselves from attack by hiding, or by making themselves look invisible. Others use stings, poisons, and other weapons.

Perfectly Adapted

Our world is freezing cold in some parts and extremely hot in others. Animals have layers of fat and thick fur to keep them warm, and other **adaptations** to keep them cool. Some rest during the day and come out in the cool of the night. To move around and find food in the dark, they have developed amazing senses that daytime animals do not need. Whatever the temperature, and whatever the surroundings, animals can live in their habitats successfully. We should celebrate this incredible diversity, or variety, in the animal kingdom.

MATH ATTACK!

The little Arctic tern is a record-breaking flier, perfectly built for its long flights.

There is one bird that makes an extraordinary journey every year. The tiny Arctic tern flies from the top of the world, the Arctic, to the bottom of the world, the Antarctic, and back again. It nests in the Arctic in summer, then flies south to feed. It returns to the Arctic to nest again. That is about 44,000 miles (71,000 km). One Arctic tern can live for 30 years. How many miles does it fly during its life? Use this calculation to help you solve the problem:

44,000 MILES X 30 YEARS = ? MILES

ANSWERS

Now that you have read about amazing animal bodies, try to learn more. Find out about the animals that live near you, in your backyard or the local park, lake, or river. Here are the answers to the Math Attack problems. How did you score?

PAGE 7:

400 TAMARINS ÷ 20 TAMARINS EACH YEAR = 20 YEARS

PAGE 11:

18-POUND ANT X 20 = 360 POUNDS MAXIMUM WEIGHT

PAGE 15:

20 FEET – 5 FEET = 15 FEET

PAGE 19:

3 + 1 + 1 + 2 = 7 ANIMALS X 5 WEEKS = 35 ANIMALS

PAGE 23:

7 DAYS A WEEK X 3 WEEKS = 21 DAYS
21 DAYS X 4 TEASPOONS = 84 TEASPOONS

PAGE 27:

44,000 MILES X 30 YEARS
= 1,320,000 MILES.
THAT IS THE SAME AS TRAVELING TO
THE MOON AND BACK 3 TIMES!

GLOSSARY

abdomen The rear part of an insect's body.

adaptations Features of an animal's body, or of its behavior, that help it survive.

antennae Long, thin stalks on a bug's head used for sensing.

birds of prey Birds that hunt other animals for food.

camouflage The way an animal blends in with its surroundings.

cold-blooded Describes an animal that is unable to make heat inside its body.

crustaceans Animals with a shell, such as crabs or lobsters.

fangs Long, sharp teeth.

habitats Places where an animal or plant lives.

mane Long hair around an animal's head.

nocturnal Describes something active at night.

predators Animals that kill or eat other animals.

prey Animal that is killed or eaten by another animal.

primates Mammals with a developed brain, eyes facing forward, a shortened nose, and thumbs that can move forward to touch the other fingers on the same hand.

pupa The hard cover a caterpillar makes around itself before it becomes a butterfly.

species A kind of living thing.

streamlined A smooth, pointed shape that cuts easily through water or air.

tentacles Long, flexible parts of the body.

thorax The middle part of an insect's body.

webbed Having toes joined by pieces of skin.

FURTHER READING

Books

Jenkins, Steve. *The Animal Book: A Collection of the Fastest, Fiercest, Toughest, Cleverest, Shyest—and Most Surprising—Animals.* Boston, MA: HMH Books for Young Readers, 2013.

Holland, Jennnifer. *Unlikely Friendships: 47 Remarkable Stories from the Animal Kingdom.* New York, NY: Workman Publishing Company, 2011.

Markle, Sandra. *What If You Had Animal Feet?* New York, NY: Scholastic, 2015.

Spelman, Lucy. *National Geographic Animal Encyclopedia.* Washington, DC: National Geographic, 2012.

Websites

Due to the changing nature of Internet links, PowerKids Press has developed an online list of websites related to the subject of this book. This site is updated regularly. Please use this link to access the list:
www.powerkidslinks.com/ma/bodies

INDEX